This edition is published by special arrangement with Candlewick Press Inc., Cambridge, MA.

Grateful acknowledgment is made to Candlewick Press Inc., Cambridge, MA, for permission to reprint *Leon and Bob* by Simon James. © 1997 by Simon James.

Printed in Singapore

ISBN 0-15-314270-7

5 6 7 8 9 10 068 02 01

LEON
AND
BOB

Simon James

 Harcourt

Orlando Boston Dallas Chicago San Diego

Visit *The Learning Site!*

www.harcourtschool.com

Leon had moved into town
with his mom.
His dad was away in the army.
Leon shared his room
with his new friend, Bob.

No one else could see Bob,
but Leon knew he was there.
Leon always laid a place
for Bob at the table.
"More milk, Bob?" Leon said.

When Leon's mom
couldn't take Leon to school,
Leon didn't mind.
He always walked to school with Bob.
He always had Bob to talk to.

Often, when Leon got home,
there was a letter waiting for him
from his dad.
Bob liked to hear Leon read it
over and over again.

One Saturday, Leon heard
some noises in the street below.
He saw a new family moving in
next door.
A boy looked up at Leon and waved.
Leon waved back.

That night Leon kept thinking
about the boy next door.
He decided to go by there
in the morning.
"But you'll have to come with
me, Bob," he said.

The next day Leon and Bob
ate their breakfast
very quickly.
Then Leon grabbed his ball
and rushed outside.

Leon ran up the steps
of the house next door.
He was about halfway
when suddenly he realized
Bob wasn't there anymore.

Leon sat down.

He was all alone.

He could ring the bell

or he could go home.

Why wasn't Bob there

to help him?

Leon rang the bell
and waited.

The door opened.

"Hello," said the boy.

"H-hello," said Leon.

"Would you like to go to the park?"

"Okay," said the boy.

"I'm just going to the park, Mom,"
he called.

Together Leon and the boy walked
down the steps toward the street.

"My name's Leon," said Leon.

"What's yours?"

"Bob," said Bob.